THE FRESHWATER EEL

FRANCINE JACOBS

drawings by Josette Gourley

WORLD'S WORK LTD
The Windmill Press
Kingswood, Tadworth, Surrey

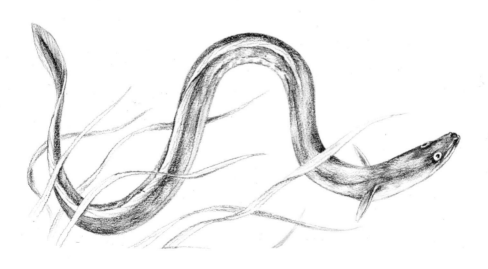

SBN 437 50151 5

BY THE SAME AUTHOR:
Sea Turtles

CONTENTS

For my mother,
and in memory of my father.

MYSTERIOUS ORIGINS

Ever since ancient times the common freshwater eel has been a mystery to man. Its long, slender shape, slimy skin, and unusual fins make it different from most fishes. Although it is a fish, the eel has been mistaken for the sea snake, and it has been confused with the "electric eel," which is not really an eel at all, but a fish that lives in certain South American rivers.

The eel family is a large one. At least three hundred kinds of eels are known, and they are found throughout the world, in warm seas and deep, cold oceans. Most eels, including the huge conger and the sharp-toothed moray, spend their entire life in the sea. Freshwater eels, however, move from one kind of water to another.

No other eel, perhaps no other animal, has kept its life cycle hidden for so long as the freshwater eel. No one ever has seen it lay eggs or bear live young. Where does it come from? How does it get born? How is it able to walk on land?

Fantastic theories have existed about this eel. Because it lives on the muddy bottom, people believed that it somehow arose from mud. Twenty-three hundred years ago, in his book the *History of Animals,* the great scientist, Aristotle, wrote that eels grow "out of the earth's guts" in mud and in moist ground.

Aristotle's theory remained unchallenged, because no one could come up with a better explanation. Indeed, those eels that were caught and examined never had eggs or fluid containing sperm. They did not have reproductive organs like those of other fishes. No wonder people believed that this eel arose magically by itself.

In the first century A.D., three hundred years after Aristotle, a highly respected Roman naturalist known as Pliny the Elder expressed what was to become another accepted theory about the eel. Pliny too believed that the eel generated itself, but he did not think that it popped out from mud. The eel had young, Pliny said, by stroking against rocks in the sea. Those pieces that broke off became infant eels and swam away.

In the sixteenth and seventeenth centuries, other peculiar ideas about the eel's origins were popular. If hairs from a horse's tail were snipped into small pieces and dropped into a river, people claimed that they would puff up and become baby eels. Other beliefs were that infant eels grew from skin shed by adults, or that they emerged from dew dropped early on a May or June morning.

Not until relatively recent times did scientists begin to discover clues to the mystery. They observed that, in the autumn, numbers of large, brown eels swam down rivers and disappeared into the sea. In the spring, young yellow eels, as long and thin as needles, appeared swimming upstream. What happened to the eel between the time the adults departed and the young arrived?

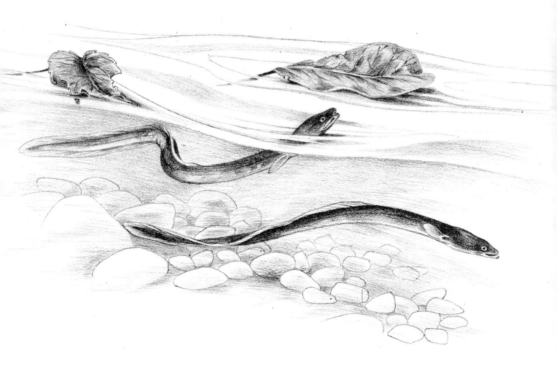

Unknowingly, Johann Kaup, a German naturalist, provided the first information in 1856. Scientist friends sent him some small, clear, ribbon-like fishes that they had netted in the Mediterranean Sea.

Never before had Kaup seen fishes such as these. They looked like tiny, transparent willow leaves, and he could see clearly through their bodies. Kaup studied them carefully and proudly described them in much detail, for he believed that he had discovered a new kind of fish. He named them *Leptocephalus brevirostris,* which in Greek means *thin head, short nose.* The name was long and impressive for a fish merely three inches long.

Unfortunately, Kaup died never knowing of his great contribution to the study of the eel. Twenty-two years after his death, in 1895, two Italian biologists, Grassi and Calandruccio, netted the same small, leaf-shaped fishes in the Mediterranean Sea and recognized them by Kaup's description. Instead of preserving them in alcohol, they placed them in a saltwater aquarium to study. To their amazement, they noticed that after several weeks the tiny fishes gradually be-

14

came glassy, needle-shaped baby eels. Kaup's fishes were not a new species at all, but the larval, or infant form, of the common eel.

Early in the nineteen hundreds another piece of evidence was provided. A Danish zoologist, Johannes Schmidt, was netting cod fry between Scotland and Iceland and scooped into his boat a three-inch eel larva. Schmidt was amazed by his find, for he had captured the first eel larva outside the Mediterranean Sea.

15

European governments were enthusiastic about Schmidt's discovery and determined to locate the eel's spawning ground. Eels always have been an important food fish for the peoples of Europe, especially in Scandinavia, so Norway and Denmark offered to provide scientists and ships for the search. Headed by Schmidt, the expedition combed the North Sea, the English Channel, the waters near France and Spain, and the Mediterranean for eel larvae. They dragged nets at every depth from the bottom of the sea to its surface, sifting tons of plankton, tiny plant and animal life, for some sign of the elusive larvae.

Year after year Schmidt went to sea. The Danish merchant fleet assisted him. The odds against finding small larvae in the open waters must have seemed overwhelming, but still they were located off the islands of the Azores in the Atlantic.

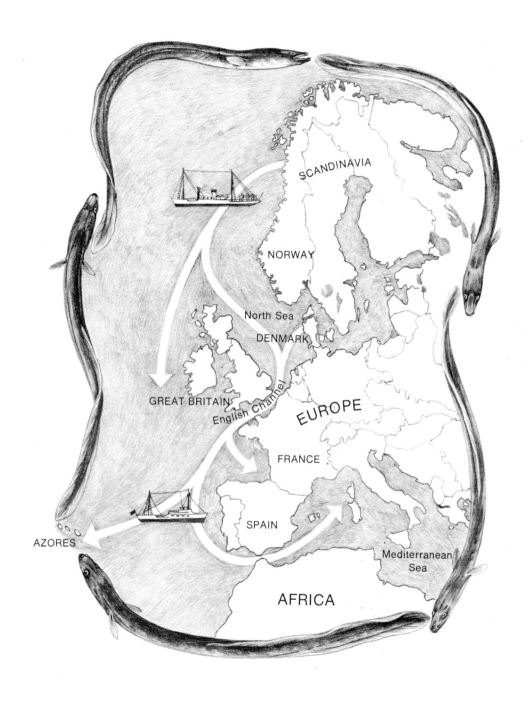

SCANDINAVIA

NORWAY

North Sea

DENMARK

GREAT BRITAIN

English Channel

EUROPE

FRANCE

SPAIN

AZORES

Mediterranean
Sea

AFRICA

The search was extended across the ocean, and Schmidt began capturing larvae regularly. He charted their size and location, and he discovered that the larvae drifted towards Europe and towards North America from the western Atlantic, increasing in size as they approached the mainland. He reasoned that the smallest larvae must be the youngest. Could this behaviour mean that European eels and North American eels come from the same spawning ground in the western Atlantic?

Finally, aboard the *Dana* in 1922, Schmidt sailed into the Sargasso Sea, south of Bermuda and east of Florida. There he found larvae only quarter of an inch long. They were netted at extreme depths and were the smallest ever seen. Beyond a doubt they were newly hatched. Schmidt had succeeded at last in locating the eel's spawning ground. His search had taken eighteen years.

The eel's birthplace, the Sargasso, isn't actually a sea. It is a deep region that is formed by currents swirling slowly in a clockwise direction around the edges of the North Atlantic. These currents bring floating masses of yellow-brown seaweed together. The area, noted by Columbus on his first voyage, was named Sargasso after a Portuguese grape because of the many grape-like pods among the weeds. Out there under this weedy carpet the eel begins its life.

20

SALTWATER YEARS

Now that the secret of the eel's birthplace was known, the story of its puzzling life cycle began to emerge. The question of how the eel has young without reproductive organs already had been solved. Eels that died and were washed ashore during the spawning journey provided the answer. On examination, scientists discovered that they had reproductive organs. Only during the long voyage, however, does this development occur.

Eels from both sides of the Atlantic

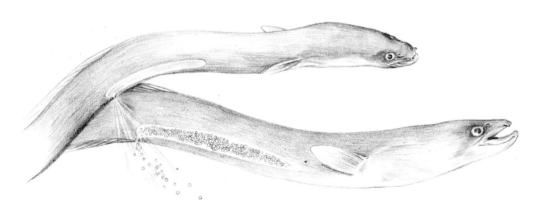

EGGS BEING FERTILIZED BY SPERM

travel to the Sargasso to mate as well as to spawn. Those from North America may travel a distance of one thousand miles or more, arriving in late winter. European eels have an even longer trip. They journey more than three thousand miles and meet in an area just slightly north of the North American eels, arriving during spring and summer.

Although the spawning grounds of the European and North American eels are thought to overlap to some extent, the two eels probably have no contact with each other. Each group spawns about twelve hundred feet below the dense Sargassum weed, as far down as the Empire State Building would reach if it were lowered into the sea. The ocean bottom, however, is still farther down, for at this point it is almost four miles deep, deeper than the height of Mount McKinley, North America's tallest mountain.

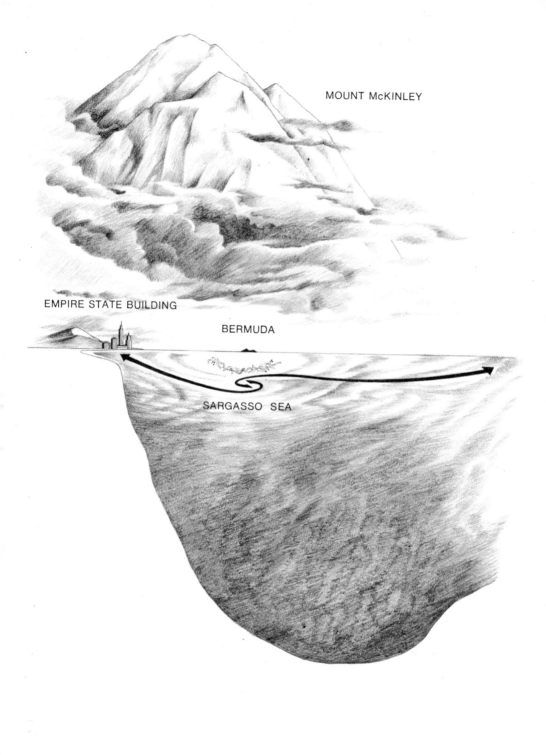

MOUNT McKINLEY

EMPIRE STATE BUILDING

BERMUDA

SARGASSO SEA

Because eels meet each other in these deep, dark depths, where no man has watched them, their mating behaviour remains uncertain. It is believed, however, that the male twists his rope-like body round the female, causing her to release eggs, which he covers with sperm. Whether one male fertilizes the eggs of one female or the eggs of many is unknown.

A large female is thought to lay as many

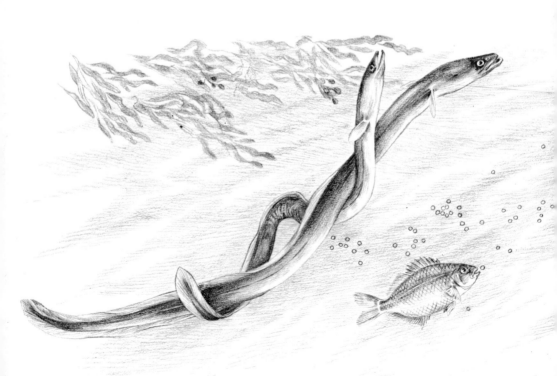

as twenty million eggs, an astounding
number for any fish to produce. But the
spawning eel does not guard her eggs,
and millions are eaten by other fishes.
Each eel egg is tiny and round, like the
head of a pin, and is transparent. It con-
tains a bit of yolk and a droplet of oil. This
oil, lighter than water, keeps the eggs
from sinking like those of many other
fishes. It is believed that the eggs take
about a week or so to hatch.

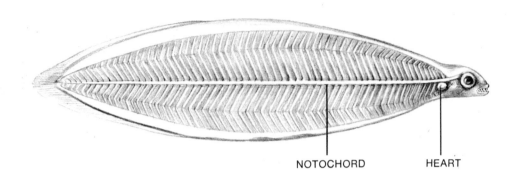

NOTOCHORD   HEART

Once hatched, the baby eel, or larva, is flat, clear, and jelly-like. It is quarter of an inch long and looks nothing like an eel, but instead resembles a finely veined willow leaf. With a magnifying glass, one can see, however, that the larva is definitely a fish. It has large, sharp teeth and two black, shiny eyes. Behind its head beats a tiny heart, and across its back is a skeleton consisting of a central rod called the notochord, which supports it.

26

Scientists believe that the new-born larvae rise slowly to the sunlit surface of the sea. There they float helplessly. How do these feeble creatures without fins for swimming travel to lands so far away? Sea currents take them on their slow and dangerous journey much as seed is carried in the wind.

For a time the larvae float northward from the Sargasso in the warm, blue Gulf Stream, drifting and feeding on the microscopic, jewel-like plants that flourish in

the spring sea. In turn, they are fed upon
by larger creatures. Shimmering herring
dart among them, gobbling them up by
the dozens. Speedy squid seize them with
their many arms and feast upon them.
Manta rays swoop down and gather the
larvae into their hungry mouths with
their huge, wing-like fins. Jellyfish grasp
larvae with long stinging tentacles. They

28

are even prey to certain shellfish that live in the weeds. If the larva were not transparent and more easily seen, it probably would have even more enemies. In any case, how many eels survive out of the billions born is yet another unanswered question. Clearly most do not, for otherwise our rivers, lakes, and ponds would be swarming with eels.

The northward drift of the Gulf Stream

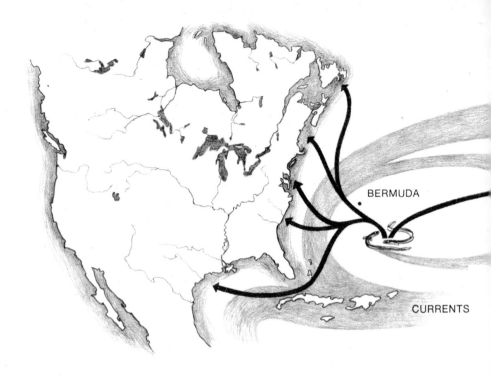

BERMUDA

CURRENTS

carries the larvae near Bermuda, where
one of the most astounding events in all
of nature occurs. In some mysterious way
the eel larvae begin to separate and to
sort themselves out. It is as if they had
arrived at a roundabout in the sea where
a policeman shows them the way. The
larvae of European parents drift eastward
with the Gulf Stream and head across the
Atlantic towards European waters. The

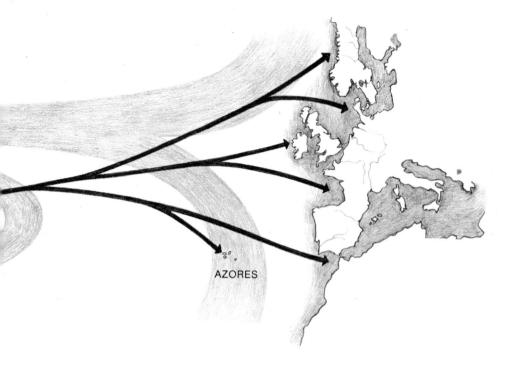

AZORES

young North American larvae appear to choose other currents, for they continue steadfastly in a northwesterly direction towards the mouths of rivers all along the Atlantic seacoast of the United States and Canada. None reach the Pacific. But how does the baby eel in its early months of life know the way to the land of its ancestors without parents to guide it and without having been there before?

31

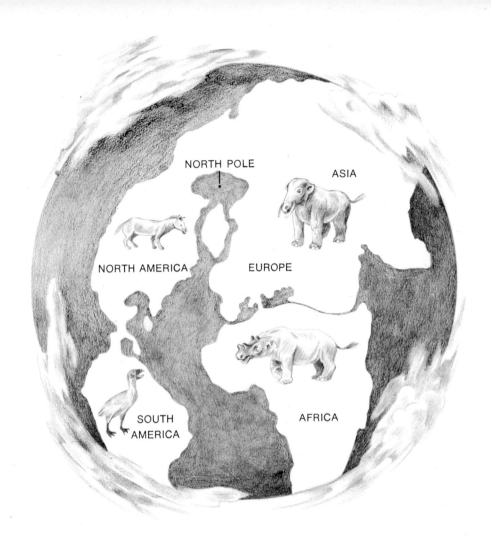

One theory claims that fifty million years ago only a narrow sea separated the coasts of Europe and North America. Probably the eel spawned in this narrow channel and made its home then, as now, in the fresh waters of the nearby continents. As the continents drifted farther and farther apart, the eel's journey lengthened. Now the baby eels need three years to reach Europe and one year to reach North America. Somehow knowledge of the route is handed down instinctively from generation to generation.

Although they look alike, there is a difference between the European and North American eel. In his search for the spawning ground, Johannes Schmidt noted that the European larva has between 111 and 118 vertebrae in its backbone while the North American species has only between 104 and 110. The eel's backbone is its passport home. By the time both species reach home waters, they are three inches in length and ready to undergo the first of the many extraordinary changes that occur to the eel during its lifetime.

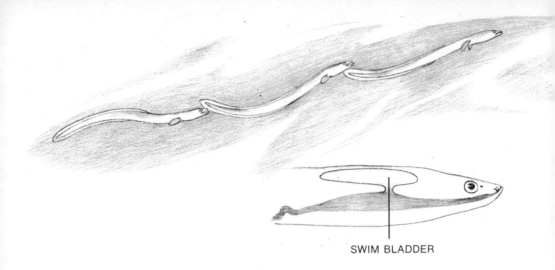

SWIM BLADDER

When the larva arrives, it is winter-time on both sides of the Atlantic. The waters are cold. As it drifts along offshore, it loses fluid and begins to shrivel. The larva shrinks from three inches to two, and its notochord is replaced by a bony skeleton. Now it is like other fishes belonging to the same order, the Teleostei. The larva loses its flat, thin appearance and slowly becomes rounder until finally it assumes the shape of an eel. Because it is still transparent, the eel at this stage of development is called a "glass" eel. It now sheds

34

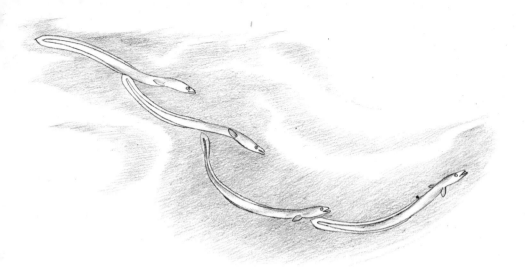

its larval teeth and uses its swim bladder.

This small, cigar-shaped organ inside the eel enables it to descend or to rise in the water. Its bladder is filled and emptied by the passage of gases between it and its bloodstream. When the bladder is emptied, the eel drops; when it is filled, the eel rises. The eel repeats this procedure many times, adjusting to changes in water pressure. During the last cold weeks of winter, the glass eel descends into deep waters to hibernate and to fast until spring.

Spring tides, rich in new plant and animal life, signal the change of season to the eel. It has very keen senses of smell and taste, tasting not only with its tongue, but with taste buds all along the sides of its body. Stirred by these senses, the eel rises and makes its way across the underwater border land known as the continental

shelf. Swimming with the incoming tide, the eel rides into coastal bays. In order not to be carried back to sea on the out-going tide, it dives down and clings to the ocean floor.

Bay water is not as salty as seawater. In it, the glass eel begins a slow and delicate process of adjustment that eventually adapts it for life in freshwater. Why the eel leaves the sea remains a secret, but some powerful instinct drives it. Gradually it moves into less and less salty water, closer and closer to shore. Now it grows its second pair of teeth and hungrily seeks food. It noses its way around pilings, under wharves, piers, and bridges, eating fishes, clams, shrimps, insects, worms, plants, and even refuse. Like the sea gull above, the eel is a scavenger feeding on every edible morsel it finds.

The young eel thrives and develops on this hotchpotch of a diet. Fins grow, and now it is able to propel itself through the water quickly and gracefully. Except for its front fins, the pectorals, which are on each side of its body behind its head, the eel's fins do not resemble those of most

other fishes. There are no separate back,
tail, and anal fins. Instead, all three are
joined together into one, long, spineless
fin that runs lengthwise like a soft fringe
from the middle of its back to its belly.
The eel also develops unusual covers that
conceal and protect its gills. It breathes
like any other fish, taking water in
through its mouth and forcing it through
its gills, where oxygen is absorbed, and
out through its gill slits.

40

FRESHWATER YEARS

Once the glass eel acquires colour in its skin, its development in brackish, ocean waters is complete. This change takes place when a tiny gland in the eel's brain, called the pituitary, is stimulated. It secretes a chemical that causes pigment or colour to appear in the eel's skin as if paint had been poured slowly into its clear body. The glass eel turns grey and then gradually yellow. At this time its lateral lines become apparent. These thin, dark lines running along both sides of its body

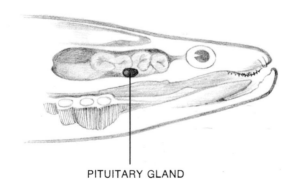

PITUITARY GLAND

LATERAL LINE

contain small pores that help the eel to hear. The eel at this stage of development is called an elver.

The elver is a little fingerling about three inches long. Now it has the slippery overcoat with which you are familiar if you ever have tried to grasp an eel. This slime, or mucus, that covers its body is very important. It keeps the eel alive during its adaptation from salt water to fresh and protects it from disease. If the eel is injured, the slime hastens healing. It reduces friction too and probably helps the eel to swim faster and to wriggle over rough surfaces.

42

When the spring rains subside and tidal waters lower, elvers in every bay and inlet push their way into the rivers. At this time, for reasons that are not known, male and female elvers separate. The males, as if obeying some ancient taboo, remain in the brackish waters, travelling back and forth from them into nearby bays and channels to search for food. The females, however, enter freshwater and swim upstream. From the Mississippi to

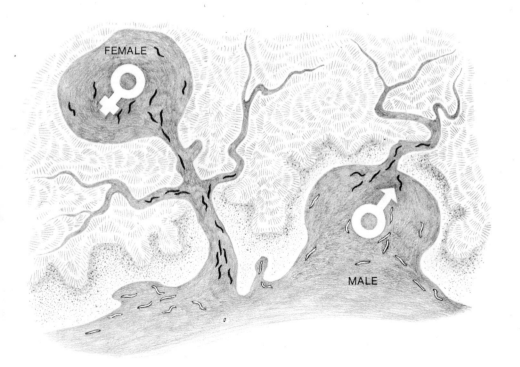

FEMALE

MALE

the Saint Lawrence, and in the rivers of
Europe, this strange rite occurs each
spring-time.

Through bustling harbours and ports,
amid the traffic of ships and barges, and
against tides of pollution, the female
elvers begin their freshwater migration.
Night and day countless elvers force their
way upstream in long unbroken chains.
They travel close to shore, so close that
people catch them by the dozens in pails,
bags, and nets. The English people on the
River Severn long ago named this re-
markable event the eel-fare. *Fare* means

to go, and the term appropriately describes the unusual passing of the elvers. In England, in Spain, and in southern France, elvers are eaten and considered such a delicacy that they are tinned and sold in shops.

Natural enemies as well as man take their toll of the elvers. Snapping turtles and birds, such as herons and kingfishers, devour them. So do freshwater fishes like bass, perch, pickerel, and pike. Even older eels eat elvers. Neither natural enemies nor physical barriers stop them, however.

The female elver has an almost unbelievable ability to overcome obstacles. She drives herself over rocks, squeezes under logs, and pushes up through waterfalls and rapids. To get around a dam, she will detour through brooks and drains. She even will travel, when necessary, through sewers. Sometimes she enters a spring and travels through an underground stream. Many a farmer has been surprised to find an elver swimming in his well water. All during the course of her freshwater journey, the eel is growing. She becomes darker in colour and turns from yellow-green to brownish-black on top, olive on the sides, and white on the belly. These colours help to camouflage her.

How the eel gets into land-locked lakes thousands of feet above sea level was a puzzle for a long time. Although eels can't fly, scientists at last learned that they

can walk. At night, when the earth is moist, the eel wriggles out of a stream and onto the land. She may slither for a mile before the morning sun forces her to hide. Wet grasses, mud, leaves, or rocks provide a suitable, damp shelter. One of the few fishes that can live out of water, the eel can survive on land up to two days as long as she keeps moist. Her mucus helps to prevent her from drying out. During this time she breathes through tiny pores in her skin.

What determines why the female chooses a particular lake, pond, stream, or creek to be her home? Is she guided by instinct? Did her mother live there? Or is she merely tired and ready to settle down? No one knows.

Having reached her goal, the female lives a quiet life. She rests in the mud during the day and spends her nights poking about the bottom searching for food. She pushes her lower jaw into holes, cracks, and crannies, eating almost anything, including snails, crayfish, young salmon, trout, and shad. She noses into the shad fish to devour its eggs and is the arch enemy of the shad fisherman.

The North American female grows to

a weight of about three and a half pounds
and an average length of one yard or
more. She is twice as long as the ordinary
male. European eels are much smaller
and only weigh about fourteen ounces.
Because of the eel's long, slender shape,
both the male and the female are able to
squirm into the strangest places. Fisher-
men have pulled them up in old boots,
pails, and pocketbooks. It is a common
but gruesome fact that eels often are
found in the bodies of the drowned.

Although a young eel has no scales,
they develop in three years' time after the

eel has left the sea. Even then they are hardly noticeable, for eel scales are tiny and are sunk in the skin. Like the rings in a cross section of tree, rings in the scales of an eel tell much about its past history. These rings form each year depending on the season. In the warm months eels feed and grow, and a wide ring develops. In the cool months they hibernate, growing only a little and producing a narrow ring.

The age of an eel can be determined by counting the rings on one of its scales. One must remember to add on the three years that the eel lived without scales in freshwater and, if it is the North American type, the one year as a larva in the ocean. If it is a European eel, it will have spent three years in the ocean.

SECTION OF SKIN
SHOWING SCALES

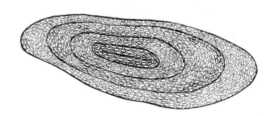

CROSS SECTION
OF SINGLE SCALE

Eels have long lives for animals. Males live an average of ten to fifteen years and return to the sea sooner than the females. The females live from twelve to twenty-two years. One eel was known to have had an unusually long life. Vadim Vladykov, an authority on eels, tells of a famous eel in Sweden named Putte, which was caught at the age of three and outlived several owners. It finally died in a museum at the age of eighty-eight.

RETURN TO THE SEA

After the eels have lived out of the sea for a number of years, some overpowering drive suddenly stirs within them and calls them back. With a sense of urgency both the male and female eels begin to eat enormous amounts of food and to store considerable fat in their body. This preparation for the spawning voyage may take as long as a year. Then, late one summer,

the reverse migration occurs. At this time
the eel turns a darker colour and develops
a metallic sheen. Now the eel is the fat,
meaty, "silver" eel that European fisher-
men seek. Because of a slight difference
in colour, the North American eel is
known as the "bronze" eel at this stage.

It is believed that once the eel begins its

journey, it lives off the stored fat and never eats again. The few specimens of eels that have died en route and been washed ashore have had no food in their stomach and their intestine was shrivelled up and withered.

As if in anticipation of a long, dark sojourn under the sea, the eel's eyes more

than double in size and become the most noticeable feature on its head. In this respect, it begins to resemble those strange fishes that are found at great ocean depths.

The female chooses a windy, rainy night in the autumn to depart. What determines the exact time is still unknown.

Perhaps she waits for the autumn rains
to swell the brooks and streams that she
must use to wend her way to the larger
rivers. Autumn storms may signal her to
expect higher tides that will help her get
to the sea.

Once under way, she swims by the same fields, farms, and cities that she passed some twenty years before. She travels at night for weeks until she reaches the river's mouth. There she must pause and readjust to the increased saltiness of the brackish waters. And there she is met by the males, which also have undergone the changes for the spawning journey. They are not the same males that accompanied her from the Sargasso Sea. They have returned to spawn already. These males are younger and left the ocean later.

By the end of November all the spawn-

ing eels are gone from the rivers and bays on both sides of the Atlantic, leaving behind those whose turn has yet to come. The eel's voyage back to the Sargasso Sea is steeped in mystery. No one knows whether they travel in groups or separately. The spawning eels are powerful swimmers unlike the helpless larvae they once were. The depth at which they swim and the route that they take also remain mysteries. Most mysterious of all is the means they use to navigate through thousands of miles of open sea back to the very place where they were born.

Do they use smell and taste to seek out the proper currents? Or do the differences in water temperature serve as a guide? Perhaps they possess some strange internal compass that we have yet to discover. Like other migratory animals, the eel spawns in the exact same ideal conditions that existed for its own birth.

The eel reaches the Sargasso Sea after months of travel, and there in the warm, salty, murky depths it produces a new generation. Having performed this duty, spent and exhausted, the eel disappears. Does it die or does it live on in those remote waters? No one knows for certain. We have learned much about the eel, yet its life in many ways still remains an enigma.